Design and Make
CLOTHES
AND SHOES

Helen Greathead

A⁺

Smart Apple Media

Contents

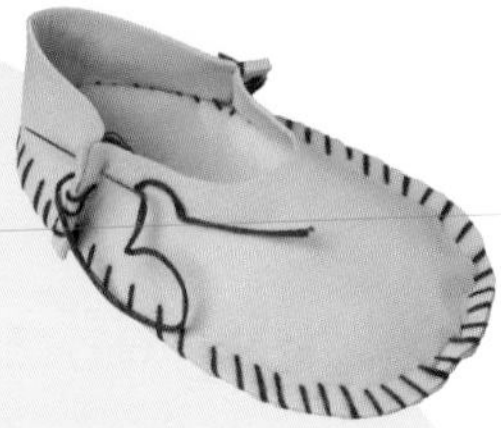

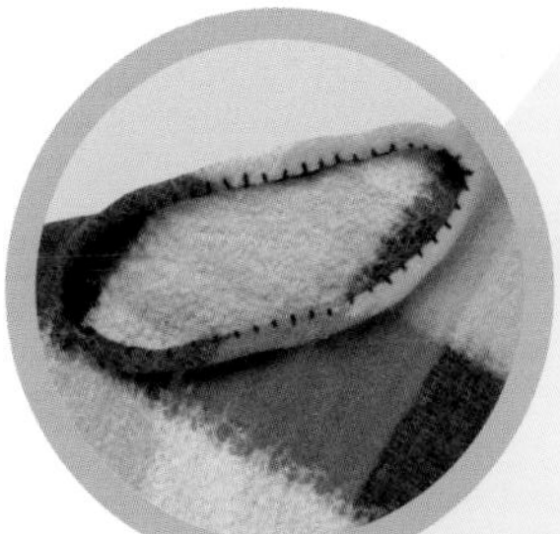

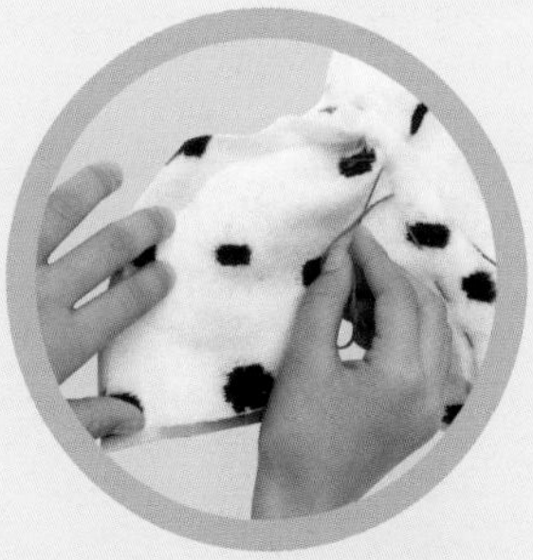

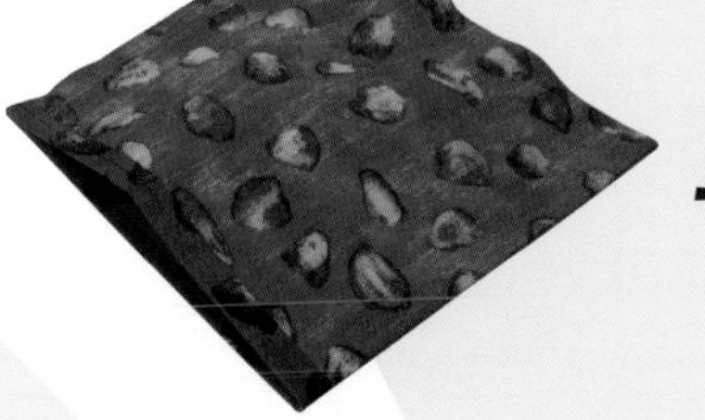

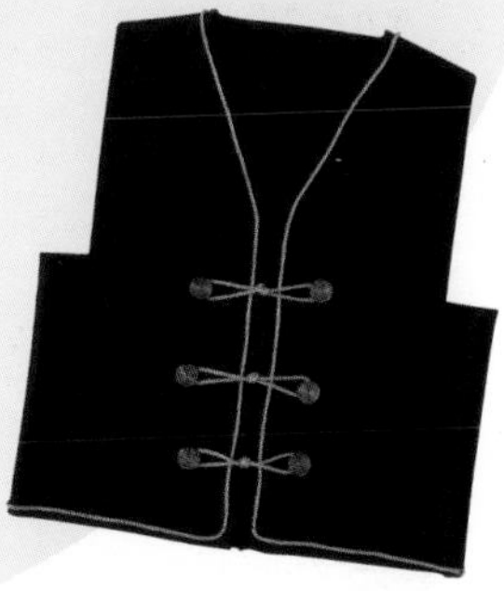

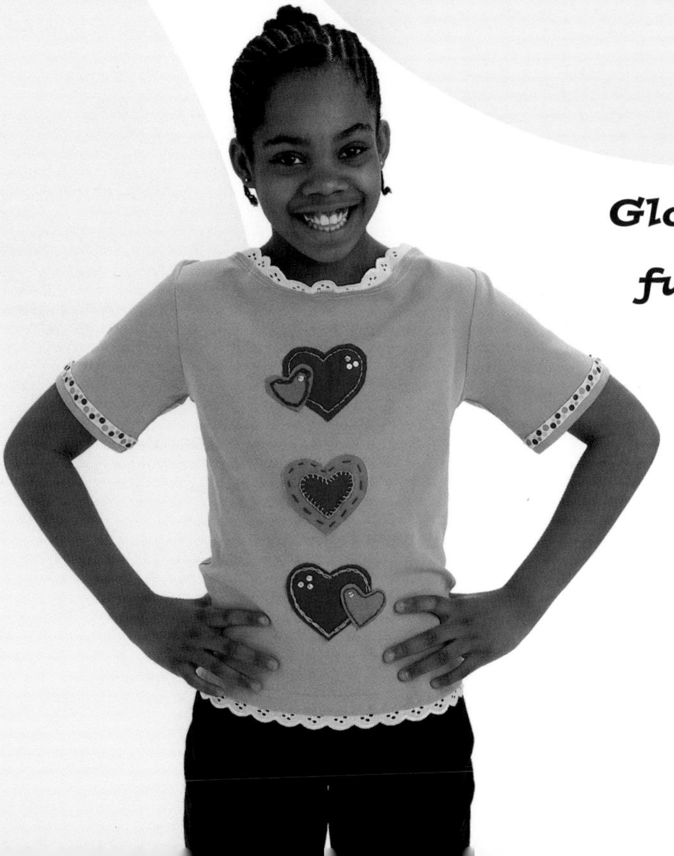

Why do we wear clothes?

People wear clothes for all sorts of reasons: to keep cool or warm, or to protect their skin from the sun, rain, and wind. Shoes, hats, and gloves protect feet, heads, and hands. But clothes are not just practical—they have become part of the way people express themselves, their cultures, and their personalities.

Simple but stylish

Clothes don't have to be complicated. In South America, the poncho is really just a blanket with a hole in it to slip over your head. In Southeast Asia, many people wear simple sarongs.

Talking kimono

In Japan, kimonos can serve different purposes. Kimono actually means "things to wear," and at one time, people in Japan had a different kimono for every occasion. Your kimono said something about you, such as how old you were or whether you were married.

What do your clothes say?

These days, we can dress more or less how we please. Our clothes often show what sort of person we are. Choose from the projects in this book and see if you can make your outfits say something about you.

A few hints and tips

Here are a few other ideas to help you get started.

Finding materials

• Ask your family and friends, or look in second-hand shops.
• Buy small quantities of material—look in the scraps box in your local fabric store.
• Always clear plenty of space to work. Fabrics are best cut on a smooth, hard surface. The floor is as good as anywhere!

Pattern-making

• Use newspaper to make patterns. Stick pieces together with masking tape. Use greaseproof paper as an alternative.
• To make a pattern that is symmetrical, fold the paper in half and draw one half of the shape you need. Then, cut across the fold through both layers of paper.
• Always allow at least half an inch (1.3 cm) for a seam unless the instructions say otherwise.
• Once you've made your pattern, pin it onto the fabric and then cut around it.

Hemming

• After you have cut the material, you will need to hem the edges to stop it from fraying. You can either hem using a simple running stitch (see page 7) or use an instant hemming adhesive (which you can buy from fabric stores and simply iron on). Always ask an adult to help you when ironing.

Be prepared

Here is a collection of things you will need to make the clothes and shoes in this book. You can collect things gradually and store them in a large box.

Getting it right

• To make sure you make your clothes and shoes the right size, it's a good idea to make a pattern first using scrap pieces of material.
• When you are ready to make your actual item, tack the material together with running stitch before you sew it. Use colorful thread to make it easier to remove the tacking afterward.

Things to collect

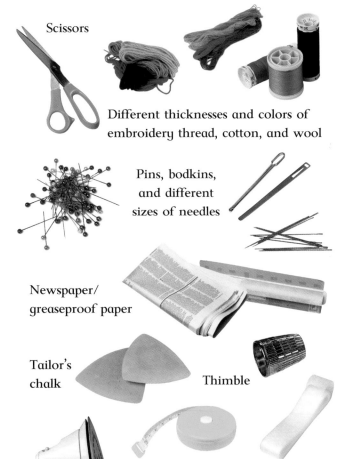

Scissors

Different thicknesses and colors of embroidery thread, cotton, and wool

Pins, bodkins, and different sizes of needles

Newspaper/ greaseproof paper

Tailor's chalk

Thimble

Tape measure   Hemming adhesive

Sewing machine and an iron and ironing board. Always ask an adult to help you use these.

Old bucket or bowl (ask before using!)

SEA SALT

Plenty of salt

Cold dyes

Rubber gloves and an apron or old shirt

Fabric paint and pens

Fabrics: old sheets, quilt covers, blankets, pajamas, curtains, clothes, scraps of material, fake fur, fake leather, felt, chamois leather, any interesting textured fabrics

Old cereal boxes and packaging

Craft glue

Double-sided tape, masking tape; duct tape

Interesting scraps of lace, ricrac, and other trimmings

Rubber bands

Ribbon

Pom-poms

Sequins

Leather thonging

Beads

Buttons

Stitches

We use different stitches for different reasons. Here are three important ones. Always begin by tying a knot in the end of your thread.

Running stitch

Push the needle through the fabric and back out again to make a neat row of stitches that look the same on both sides. Use small running stitches for hemming, too. Use a larger version of running stitch to tack things loosely together so that you can try them on for size.

Overstitching

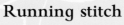

Overstitching is ideal for joining two raw edges of material together. Holding the edges together, push the needle up from the bottom and pass over the edge and up through the material again.

Blanket stitch

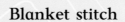

Blanket stitch is useful for binding raw edges (see page 21). Working in from the edge of the garment, push the needle through and up to the edge. Wind the thread around the needle. Pull the needle through and push it in again.

A simple sarong

A sarong is easy to make, and it's stylish, too.

Challenge
How many different ways could you wear a sarong?

Look at this!

A sarong is a piece of fabric that wraps around your body. These days, many people wear them! The pattern gives the sarong its style.

✳ How do you think the sarong is tied?

✳ Why are sarongs practical?

Design and select

Make a tie-dyed sarong for yourself. Think about the pattern you want to create and the color you will use. Which fabric will you choose? We cut up an old, white cotton sheet and used rubber bands and cold dye, with plenty of salt, to color it.

Make

1 Cut out a rectangle of fabric as wide as your outstretched arms that reaches from your armpits down past your knees. Hem the top and bottom edges only (see page 5).

2 Make sure your fabric is completely clean, then wet it thoroughly. Hold the fabric up by the center and tie rubber bands all the way down, leaving four inches (10 cm) between each one.

Challenge
How can you create a different tie-dye pattern?

3 You should wear an apron or old shirt and rubber gloves when you're using dye. Carefully follow the instructions enclosed with your dye to color the fabric—ask an adult to help you. When colored, put the dyed fabric in a plastic bag and tie it shut. Leave it somewhere warm for two hours. This will make your pattern stronger.

Challenge
How could you dye your sarong two different colors?

4 Take out your sarong and remove the rubber bands. Open it and hang it up to dry. When dry, snip the sides to create a fringe and admire your design! How will you wear your new sarong?

Customize a T-shirt

You don't always have to make new clothes from scratch. Decorating a plain T-shirt is easy, and it looks great, too!

Design and select

Use a plain T-shirt to make a girl's decorated top. What will you use to decorate it? Draw a sketch of your ideas. Cut out samples of fabric. We used scraps of patterned fabric, embroidery, and sequins.

Challenge
How would you customize a boy's T-shirt?

Make

1 Most plain T-shirts have a high neckline. If yours does, use tailor's chalk to draw around the edge of a plate to make a lower neckline. Draw the neckline higher at the back. Carefully cut along your chalk line.

Challenge
Turn a plain T-shirt into a tank-top.

2 Try the T-shirt on inside out. If it is too long, mark the length you want with chalk. Take the T-shirt off and mark a straight line all the way around. Cut off along the line and hem carefully.

3 Tack some embroidery onto the neckline and around the bottom of the T-shirt. Sew in place with two neat lines of running stitch (see page 7).

4 Cut out shapes from different fabrics and arrange them on your T-shirt. Ask for help to use an iron to attach them with hemming adhesive, or sew them on with one of the stitches on page 7.

Challenge

How would you customize a pair of jeans?

5 Sew on any other decorations you want, such as sequins or buttons. Finish off each sleeve by sewing on a fabric band, and show off your T-shirt design!

Fisherman's trousers

These simple, baggy trousers are worn by fishermen in Thailand!

Design and select

Make a pair of colorful trousers without complicated fastenings—you can just tie a knot in the top of these to hold them up! Draw some sketches of your ideas. How long will they be? What fabric will you use? We've used a sheet from a second-hand shop.

Make

1 Sit across the fold of a large sheet of folded newspaper with your legs apart, as shown. Draw small dashes around the inside of your leg to your ankle, then around the outside of your leg to just past your waist. Ask a friend to help if you can't reach that far!

Challenge
How could you add a belt?

2 Draw a solid line one inch (2.5 cm) around the outside edge of the dashed line to give enough room for a seam. Cut out your pattern. Unfold the paper and use it to cut out two trouser shapes in your chosen fabric.

Challenge
How could you make your trousers baggier?

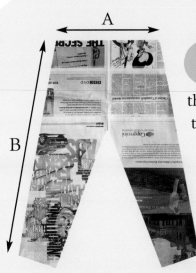

A

B

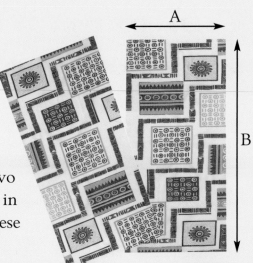

A

B

3 Measure the pattern across the top and along the outside leg.

4 Cut out two rectangles in your fabric to these measurements.

5 Making sure you keep the patterned sides together, tack and then sew the pieces like this:

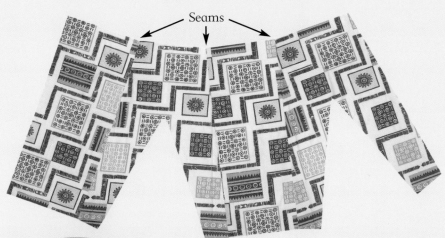

Seams

6 Tack and then sew the outer edges together and around the inside leg. Snip into the curve (see page 15). Hem the top and bottom of the trousers. Now turn them the right way out and try them on. Tie, wrap, or roll them up to fit!

Challenge
Adapt this pattern to make a pair of drawstring trousers or some overalls!

Fun fur hat

A fun fur hat will really warm you up in the winter.

Design and select

Make a fun fur hat for yourself. Look at different types of material you could use and draw some designs. We used leopard-print fake fur!

Challenge
What other fabrics would keep you warm?

Look at this!

In some parts of the world, people wear real fur to keep warm. This man lives in Tibet, where temperatures fall below 32°F (0°C).

✳ What sort of fur do you think his hat is made from?

✳ What do you think it feels like?

Make

1 Wrap a tape measure around your head, across the tops of your ears. Push two fingers inside the tape measure so that your hat will not be too tight. Read the length of the tape and add an extra inch (2.5 cm) to this measurement to allow for the seams.

Challenge
How could you give your hat a brim?

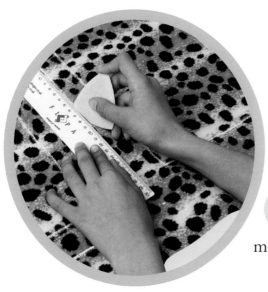

2 Use tailor's chalk and a ruler to mark two strips of fur, each half the width of your measurement and about nine inches (23 cm) high.

14

3 With the material right-sides together, tack the sides to make a tube. Try on the hat to see if it is big enough. Sew up the sides.

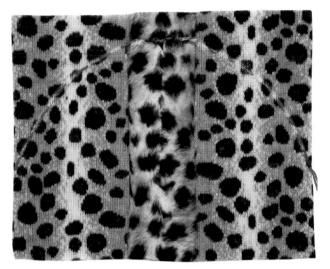

4 Flatten out the hat so that the seams are in the middle, and draw a curved line across the hat with tailor's chalk. Tack along the line and try it on again to check the size.

Challenge
How could you add earflaps to keep your ears warm, too?

5 When your hat is the right size, sew along the curve and remove the tacking stitches. Trim off any excess material. Carefully snip into the fur on the curve, as shown below. Turn your hat the right way out and put it on!

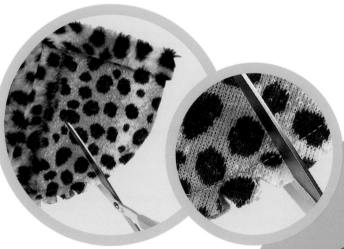

Challenge
How could you make a summer hat with a brim?

Bouncy flip-flops

Make some flip-flops to
put a spring in your step!

Design and select

Make a pair of flip-flops using everyday
materials. Sketch out some ideas and
experiment with fabric scraps to find the
best combinations. We used dress fabric
and leather thonging. The sole is made
from bubblewrap and thick cardboard.

Challenge
How could you decorate
plain, ready-made flip-flops?

Look at this!

People wear flip-flops all over
the world. They are ideal for
wearing in hot countries.

✱ Why do you think they
are so popular?

✱ What materials are used
to make them?

Make

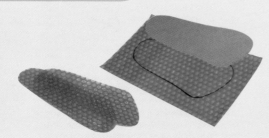

1 Draw around your right foot on a piece of
cardboard, adding an extra five millimeters
all the way around. This is the pattern for your flip-
flop. Use it to cut out six layers of bubblewrap and
two pieces of cardboard.

2 Stick the six layers of bubblewrap together
with craft glue and then sandwich them
between the top and bottom layers of cardboard, as shown.

3 Cut out a piece of fabric using the pattern, adding
an extra 1.5 inches (4 cm) all the way around.
Turn the pattern over and cut out a second piece of
fabric, exactly the same size as the pattern, for the sole.

4 Cut two small disks of fake leather and make a
hole in the middle of each with a sharp pencil.

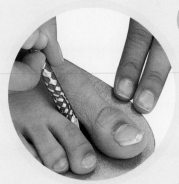

5 Place your foot on top of the cardboard and bubblewrap sole and mark between your big toe and second toe. Use your mark as a guide to make a hole all the way through with a pencil. Make a hole in the same place on the larger piece of fabric, too.

6 Loop a piece of leather thong and thread the loop through the bubblewrap sandwich. Push one fake leather disk over the loop at the top and one over the ends at the bottom. Glue both disks down in place on the cardboard.

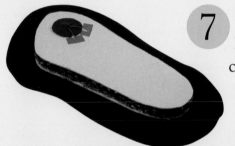

7 Push the thong through the hole in the large piece of fabric cut in step 3, leaving about a one-inch (2.5 cm) loop. Trim the ends of the thong on the bottom of the flip-flop and tape them down.

8 Fold the material down and glue it to the bottom of the flip-flop, cutting small slits as you go to make this easier.

9 Push a folded piece of dress fabric through the leather thong loop and place your foot on the flip-flop. Pull the fabric tight and tuck it under the sole. Glue down the ends.

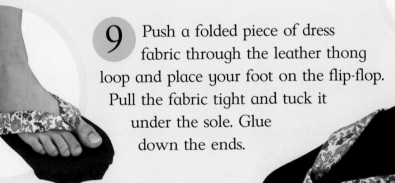

10 Make sure everything is glued down flat and neatly on the sole, then glue the smaller piece of fabric you cut in step 3 to the bottom to finish it off. Decorate the edge of the flip-flop with ricrac. Repeat these steps with your left foot to make the second flip-flop.

17

Baby slippers

Make some soft, comfortable slippers for a baby you know.

Design and select

Make and decorate a pair of soft moccasins suitable for a baby. Draw some basic slipper shapes and attach fabrics and accessories to try out ideas. We used fake leather material and pom-poms. You could use felt instead.

Look at this!

These moccasins are really comfortable to wear.

✱ What material do you think they are made from?

Make

1 Draw around the baby's foot on a sheet of paper to make the pattern. Draw another line around the foot shape, adding half an inch (1.3 cm) for the seam. Round off the toe to make the shape symmetrical.

Seam allowance →

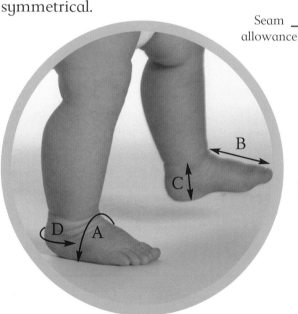

2 Cut out a shape like the one below. Measure the baby's instep—line A. Make line B as long as B on the baby's foot. Add a half-inch (1.3 cm) seam all the way around.

Seam allowance →

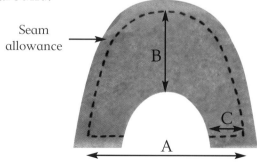

Challenge
Use this method to make slippers for yourself!

3 Use masking tape to gently attach your pattern to the fake leather and cut out carefully.

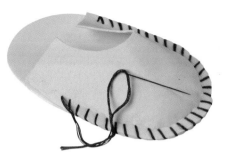

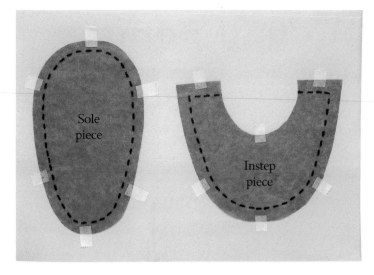

Sole piece

Instep piece

4 Use embroidery thread to sew the instep to the sole by overstitching (see page 7). Measure around the baby's heel (D) and line C (see page 18) and draw a rectangle as shown, right, adding a half-inch (1.3 cm) seam. Cut out carefully.

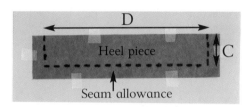

D

Heel piece

C

Seam allowance

5 Sew the heel piece to the sole. Stitch up the sides to join the heel and instep. Turn the right way out.

6 Decorate the front of the slippers with pieces of your material, and snip the sides to make a fringe. Sew on some pom-poms and the extra material with bright thread. Cut out an extra strip of material to go around the heel, and stitch it on. Have the baby try her new slippers!

Challenge
Decorate the slippers to look like a flower or a lion's face.

A cozy poncho

A poncho is really simple to make. It's easy and fun to wear, too!

Design and select

Design a poncho from warm, woven fabric. Find pictures of ponchos, traditional and modern, and make up a collage of your ideas. What fabric will you use? Will you add any decorations? We cut up an old blanket!

Make

1 Hold your arms out to the side and ask for help to measure from one wrist to the other. Use this measurement to mark two diagonal lines on your material and join up the edges to make a square. Cut out your material. Make a mark in the center.

Challenge
How could you knit your own poncho?

← 10 in →

2 Fold the blanket in half diagonally. Draw a line 10 inches (25 cm) long that cuts through the middle of your central mark along the fold. This is the hole for your head.

20

3 Use blanket stitch (see page 7) in a matching color wool to hem the neckline.

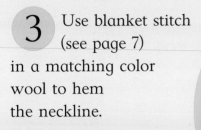

Challenge
Could you add a collar or hood?

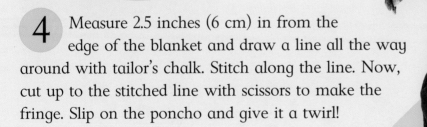

4 Measure 2.5 inches (6 cm) in from the edge of the blanket and draw a line all the way around with tailor's chalk. Stitch along the line. Now, cut up to the stitched line with scissors to make the fringe. Slip on the poncho and give it a twirl!

Challenge
How could you make tassels or add decorations such as beads?

Furry moonboots

These boots won't protect you from snow, but they make great slippers!

Design and select

Make a fun pair of moonboots. Draw boot shapes on paper and glue on different textured fabrics. Which do you like best? We used spotted fake fur, thick foam, and cardboard. Follow the steps below using scrap materials before you make the finished boots.

Look at this!

All over the world, people have designed amazing boots for harsh winter weather.

✱ What do you think these boots are made from?

✱ How are they decorated?

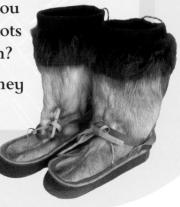

Make

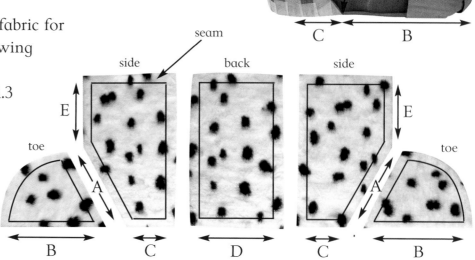

1 Stand on a piece of cardboard, draw around your foot, and cut out. Cut out a piece of foam the same size. Put your foot on the foam and make the heel and toe shapes shown below by wrapping strips of cardboard around your foot. Place another piece of cardboard over the end of the toe and secure with masking tape.

A is from the top of your foot to the side of your heel

2 Cut out your fabric for the boot following the pattern shown, adding a half-inch (1.3 cm) seam. Use the measurements from the inner shoe you made. Decide the leg height of your boots—line E.

seam

side   back   side

toe   toe

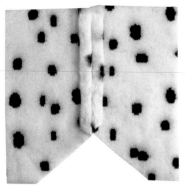

3 Sew the side pieces together along edge E with right-sides together, as shown.

Challenge
Could you use two or more fabrics?

4 Stitch the back piece (D) to the side pieces you just sewed (above), with right-sides together, to form a tube. Sew the two toe pieces together along the curved edge and then attach to the tube along the edge A (right).

5 Cut out a sole using your inner shoe as a pattern. Stitch the sole to the rest of the boot with right-sides together. Hem the top of the boot. Turn the right way out.

6 Cut another sole out of fake leather and attach it to the sole of the boot. Repeat all these steps to make the other boot. Put the cardboard inner shoes in and your boots are ready!

Challenge
How could you decorate the boots?

23

A dressing gown

Make a summer dressing gown that's like a Japanese kimono!

Design and select

Design a summer kimono with a simple belt. Draw kimono outlines. What fabric will you choose? Will you add any decorations? We used an old quilt cover and pillow cases.

Look at this!

In Japan, women's kimonos are made from beautiful printed silks. Men's summer kimonos are much simpler and made from cotton.

* What shapes make up the kimono?

* How do you think they are fastened?

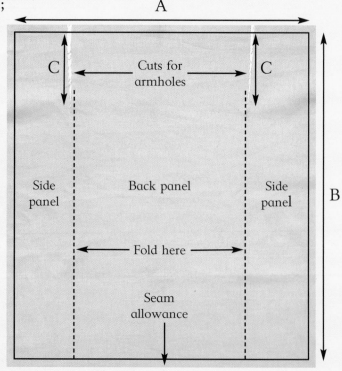

Make

1 To make the pattern for your kimono, figure out the following measurements: elbow to elbow (A); shoulder to knee (B); shoulder to elbow (C).

2 Draw a rectangle on a large sheet of newspaper. The length is measurement B and the width is A. Add half an inch (1.3 cm) all the way around for the seam and cut out. Pin it onto your fabric and cut out carefully. Make a slit at each shoulder for the arm hole; this is length C, as shown (right).

Challenge
Add a Japanese symbol with fabric paint.

A

C — Cuts for armholes — C

Side panel — Back panel — Side panel

Fold here

Seam allowance

B

3 Fold the side panels onto the back panel so that the seams line up. Tack and then sew together at the shoulders, leaving about two inches (5 cm) unstitched near the neck. Make sure the material is right-sides together.

C

seam allowance

2xC

4 Cut out your sleeves from one of the old pillow cases. Use line C for the width and twice that for the length; add an extra half-inch (1.3 cm) for the seams. Hem the outside length of each sleeve. Fold each sleeve in half, right-sides together, and sew up the top seam.

5 Lay the kimono out with the sleeves in place. (Gown and sleeves should be inside out.) Tack and then sew the top of each sleeve into the kimono, as shown.

6 Hem the rest of the sleeves and across the neck, front pieces, and bottom.

Challenge
Make a dressing gown with long sleeves.

7 To make the belt, measure around your waist and cut out a long strip of material twice this length and about 16 inches (40 cm) wide. Stitch right-sides together to make a tube, leaving one end open. Turn the right way out and overstitch the end.

Pirates ahoy!

Most children love playing pirates. Why not create a pirate outfit for a little brother or sister—or for yourself!

Design and select

Design a complete pirate costume from things you can find at home. Find some pictures of pirates and sketch out your idea. Which fabrics will you use? We chose blue felt, gold buttons, and braid for the vest, a sheet for the trousers, and rayon for the belt and scarf.

Make

Vest

Challenge
How could you make a pirate hat?

1 Fold a T-shirt in half and place it on two folded sheets of newspaper, as shown. Draw around the T-shirt.

2 Adapt your T-shirt shape to make a vest outline, adding on half an inch (1.3 cm) extra for the seam. Draw an L-shaped armhole, square off the neck, and raise the bottom edge.

3 Unfold the newspaper and cut out the patterns. Pin one pattern to a large piece of felt for the back.

T-shirt shape

Vest outline

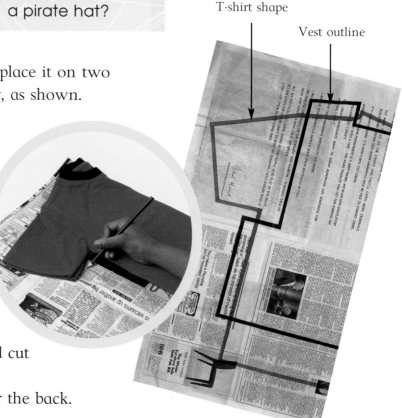

4 Fold the second piece in half again and cut a diagonal line to make the V-neckline, as shown below. Cut the pattern in half at the fold. Pin to the felt and cut out all three pieces.

5 Tack and then sew together at the shoulders and sides. Ask for help to flatten the seams with an iron. Turn your vest the right way out. Sew on buttons and braid around the edges of the vest.

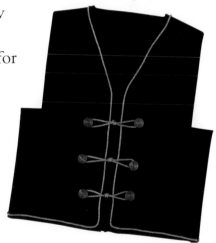

Trousers

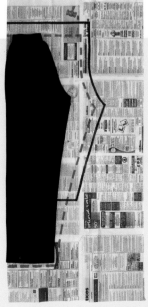

1 Lay a pair of trousers folded in half on a folded sheet of newspaper with the front of the trousers along the fold. Use the shape of the trousers to draw your pattern. Add about an inch (2.5 cm) extra at the sides to make your pirate trousers a bit baggier.

2 Now, draw your pirate trousers shape, adding an inch (2.5 cm) for the seam. Mark the length you want them to be.

3 Cut out the newspaper shape, unfold it, and use it to cut out two pieces in your trouser material.

4 Cut zig-zag shapes across the bottom of the trousers and snip again at the top of the cut like this to stop the material from fraying (left).

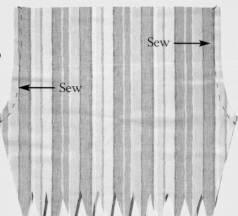

5 Place the two trouser pieces right-sides together and stitch along the curved edge, as shown (right). Ask an adult to help you iron the seams flat.

6 Fold your trousers so that the seams are now in the middle. Sew the remaining edge along the crotch, as shown (right). Trim any extra fabric and cut into the curved seam (see page 15).

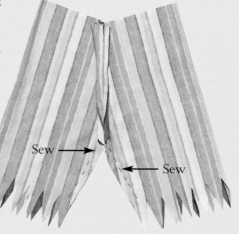

7 Fold the waistband edge down about an inch (2.5 cm) and ask an adult to help you iron this flat. Sew along this seam to make a tube for the elastic. Leave an opening of about two inches (5 cm) to thread the elastic through.

8 Cut a piece of medium elastic long enough to go around your waist, with four inches (10 cm) extra. Use a safety pin to thread the elastic through the waistband. Pin the other end to the trousers as you're doing this so it doesn't get lost.

9 When the elastic is through, pin the two ends together. Turn the trousers the right way out and try on to determine how tight the elastic needs to be. Cut and stitch the elastic together. Sew up the waistband.

Challenge

Could you make a toy sword or dagger for your pirate?

Belt

Cut a strip of fabric for the belt long enough to wrap twice around your pirate's waist. Fold the fabric in half along the length, right-sides together. Sew along the edge, cut zig-zag ends, as shown, and turn the right way out.

Headscarf

Cut a triangle of fabric. Make sure it's big enough to tie around your pirate's head. Hem around the edges.

Challenge

Adapt this outfit to make a costume for a handsome prince.

Glossary

bodkin
a blunt, thick needle used to thread elastic or tape

braid
woven thread used as trim

collage
an arrangement of different materials, such as paper or fabric, glued to a backing

embroidery thread
thick thread used to embroider

fix (ref dyeing)
to stop the color from washing out

fray
to become undone at the edges of the material

hemming adhesive
adhesive tape that is ironed on to hem material

pattern
paper or material used as a guide for shaping and cutting things that can be used more than once

right-sides
the side of the material you want showing when you wear it

ricrac
flat, narrow braid woven in zigzag form

symmetrical
a shape that can be divided in half so that one side is a mirror image of the other

thimble
a small metal or rubber cap worn on your finger to protect it when sewing

wrong-sides
the side of material you don't want showing when you wear it

Further information

You might find these Web sites helpful for finding ideas, techniques, and materials:

www.lacma.org
Los Angeles County Museum of Art, Los Angeles. Contains an online gallery of historical costumes and textiles, as well as paintings and other works of art.

www.metmuseum.org
The Metropolitan Museum of Art, New York City. Their permanent collection includes The Costume Institute, which contains historical fashions and accessories from around the world.

www.batashoemuseum.ca
The Bata Shoe Museum, Toronto, Canada. All about shoes. Contains ethnic, historical, and famous footwear.

www.museumofcostume.co.uk
Museum of Costume, Bath, England. Another costume collection—test your knowledge with some fun fashion activities.

www.pbskids.org/zoom/ activities/do
Activities section includes several fun clothes and accessories projects.

www.japanesekimono.com
To find information on kimonos, including history and facts.

www.kinderart.com/textiles/ easytiedye.shtml
For more tie-dye ideas.

www.kirbymountain.com/rosenla ke/sarong.html
To find out how to tie a sarong.

www.sherwoodsspirit.com
To look at more wonderful moccasin designs.

www.vam.ac.uk
V&A museum, London. A lot of fashion and textile ideas.

Every effort has been made by the publishers to ensure that these Web sites are suitable for children and contain no inappropriate or offensive material. However, because of the nature of the Internet, it is impossible to guarantee that the contents of these sites will not be altered. We strongly advise that Internet access is supervised by a responsible adult.

Index

First published in 2005 by
Franklin Watts, 96 Leonard Street
London EC2A 4XD

Franklin Watts Australia
Level 17/207 Kent Street, Sydney, NSW 2000

This edition published under license from Franklin Watts. All rights reserved.

Copyright © 2005 Franklin Watts

Editor: Rachel Tonkin; Art Director: Jonathan Hair;
Design: Matthew Lilly and Anna-Marie D'Cruz;
Photography: Steve Shott.
Picture credits: Alaska Stock/Alamy: 22t. Apis/Abramis/Alamy: 8t. Tizianna &
Gianni Baldizzone/Corbis: 4tr, 20t. Comstock/Alamy: 18bl. Maurice Joseph/Alamy: 14t.
Ian Masterton/Alamy: 24tc. Photo Japan/Alamy: 4bl, 24tr. Joseph Sohm/Alamy: 18tr.

Published in the United States by Smart Apple Media
2140 Howard Drive West, North Mankato, Minnesota 56003

U.S. publication copyright © 2007 Smart Apple Media
International copyright reserved in all countries. No part of this book may
be reproduced in any form without written permission from the publisher.
Printed in the United States of America

Library of Congress Cataloging-in-Publication Data

Greathead, Helen.
Clothes and shoes / by Helen Greathead.
p. cm. – (Design and make)
Includes index.
ISBN-13 : 978-1-58340-956-5
1. Children's clothing—Juvenile literature. I. Title.
II. Design and make (North Mankato, Minn.)

TT635.G74 2006
646.4—dc22   2005052553

2 4 6 8 9 7 5 3 1